# Grade Two

## Music Theory

### 4th Imprint

(ABRSM 2020+ Syllabus)

# GRADE TWO MUSIC THEORY COURSE AND EXERCISES

By Victoria Williams

www.mymusictheory.com

# CONTENTS

# INTRODUCTION

This book was written for students who are preparing to take the ABRSM Grade Two Music Theory exam. Parents of younger students will also find it helpful, as well as busy music teachers who are trying to fit a lot of music theory teaching into a very short time during instrumental lessons.

This updated 2nd edition has been revised to reflect minor changes to the ABRSM syllabus effective from 1st January 2018.

Each topic is broken down into digestible steps, and for best results the lessons should be followed in the order they are presented, as the acquired knowledge is cumulative.

After each topic, you will find a page or so of practice exercises, to help you consolidate what you have learned. Answers are provided on the page following the exercises.

At the end of the book there is a practice test which is in a similar style to the actual exam papers.

Further tests for Grade Two candidates are also available in "10 Grade Two Tests" by the same author. These comprise a set of ten score-based revision tests.

I also highly recommend purchasing ABRSM past papers before sitting an actual exam. These can be obtained from shop.abrsm.org, Amazon or your local sheet music reseller.

You are welcome to photocopy the pages of this book for your own use, or to use with your pupils if you are a music teacher.


## ABOUT THE AUTHOR

Victoria Williams graduated with a BA Hons degree in Music from the University of Leeds, UK, in 1995, where she specialised in notation and musicology. She also holds the AmusTCL and LmusTCL Diplomas in Music Theory from Trinity College London.

In 2007 she created the website www.mymusictheory.com, which initially offered free lessons for Grade 5 ABRSM Music Theory candidates. Over the years, the full spectrum of ABRSM theory grades has been added, making MyMusicTheory one of the only websites worldwide offering a comprehensive, free, music theory training programme aligned with the ABRSM syllabuses.

You can connect with Victoria Williams in the following ways:

www.mymusictheory.com

info@mymusictheory.com

www.facebook.com/mymusictheory

www.twitter.com/mymusictheory

https://www.youtube.com/user/musictheoryexpert

# 1. NOTES, RESTS AND LEDGER LINES

Here are the most common note and rest values.

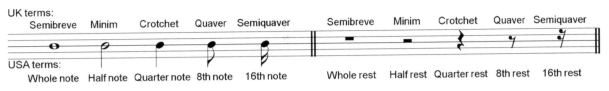

If a note or rest is **dotted** (has one dot on the right side of the note head), its length is increased by 50%. For example, a dotted minim (half note) is worth 3 crotchets (quarter notes).

The semibreve (whole) rest is also used a **full bar rest** in any time signature. It represents one bar of silence, whatever the time signature is.

## TIES IN MUSIC

**Ties** join notes of the same pitch together to make them longer. (Don't confuse ties with slurs - ties join together two notes which are the same pitch!)

## LEDGER LINES

Middle C has one ledger line, both in the treble clef, and in the bass clef.

We can add more ledger lines to the top or bottom of the stave to make more space. Let's add some ledger lines to the top of the staff in the treble clef. The first note we use a ledger line on is the A.

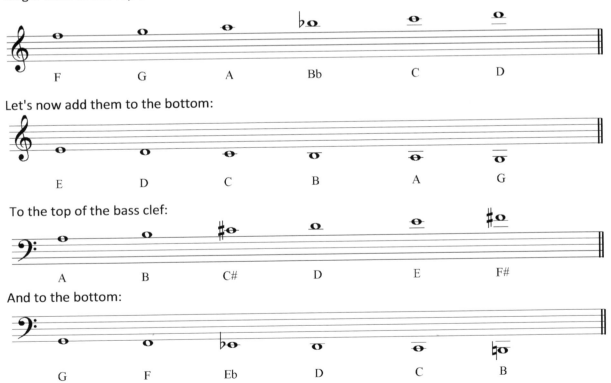

Let's now add them to the bottom:

To the top of the bass clef:

And to the bottom:

In Grade Two Music Theory, you will need to be able to read notes written with up to 2 ledger lines.

# 1. NOTES, RESTS AND LEDGER LINES EXERCISES

## EXERCISE 1

Give the letter name of each of these notes, including any sharp/flat sign when necessary.

## EXERCISE 2

Name the highest and lowest notes in each of these melodies.

Highest:                    Lowest:

Highest:                    Lowest:

## EXERCISE 3

Add the missing rests to this melody, at the places marked with a star.

# 1. NOTES, RESTS AND LEDGER LINES ANSWERS

## EXERCISE 1

a. C
b. G flat
c. A sharp
d. B
e. D flat
f. B flat
g. A
h. C sharp
i. E
j. D
k. C
l. E flat
m. C sharp
n. F sharp
o. D sharp
p. B

## EXERCISE 2

Highest: F sharp; Lowest: E

Highest: B flat; Lowest: A

## EXERCISE 3

# 2. TREBLE AND BASS CLEF
## WHAT'S NEW IN GRADE TWO

Hopefully you don't have too much difficulty working out where the notes are in treble and bass clef, as this is covered in grade one.

In the grade two music theory exam, you need to be able to **rewrite** a melody in a **different** clef - from treble to bass or from bass to treble, **without changing the pitch of the music.**

## PITCH

What is pitch? The **pitch** of a note means how high or low it is. We have many notes called "C", for example.

Look at these three Cs - they are all at different **pitches**:

On the other hand, these two Cs are at the **same pitch** although they are written in different clefs:

In the same way these pairs of notes are also at the same pitch although they are in a different clef:

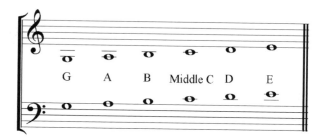

Let's look at the kind of questions you might get in the Grade Two Music Theory Exam.

The question could ask you to rewrite **single notes** with a new clef, or to rewrite a **whole melody**.

Here's a question asking you to rewrite the whole melody:

*Rewrite this melody in the treble clef, keeping the pitch the same. The first two notes are given.*

You need to write the correct notes of course, but also make sure your handwritten music is neat!

Copy each note into its new position right underneath the original melody - that way you'll make sure your notes are spaced correctly, and it's also easier to check that you haven't missed a note out by mistake!

Another useful tip is to write the last note first. Work this note out **very** carefully, and write it on your blank staff. If you make a small mistake in the middle of the melody, you will notice it more easily when you get to the end if things don't match up.

So, first, we'll put the last note in. It's the G below middle C:

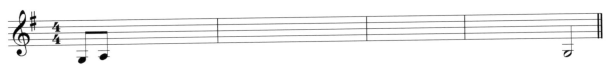

Now, start from the beginning. You don't need to spend time working out every note - just look at the general pattern. For example, for each note just say to yourself "next line up" or "2 spaces down" and so on.

When you have groups of quavers (eighth notes) or semiquavers (sixteenth notes), draw **all** the note heads in each group first. Next draw the first and last stems in each group, and finally add the beams and any other stems - and use a ruler! Pay attention to the direction of the stems - notes below the middle line have stems pointing upwards, and notes above the middle line should have stems pointing downwards.

Here's the finished answer:

## 2. TREBLE AND BASS CLEFS EXERCISES

### EXERCISE 1

Rewrite these treble clef notes in the bass clef, keeping the pitch the same. The first answer is given.

### EXERCISE 2

Rewrite these melodies in the bass clef, keeping the pitch the same. The first two notes are given.

EXERCISE 3

Rewrite these bass clef notes in the treble clef, keeping the pitch the same. The first answer is given.

EXERCISE 4

Rewrite these melodies in the treble clef, keeping the pitch the same. The first two notes are given.

## 2. TREBLE AND BASS CLEF ANSWERS

EXERCISE 1

EXERCISE 2

EXERCISE 3

EXERCISE 4

# 3. MAJOR SCALES

Major scales are built from tones and semitones, with the pattern TTS TTTS. (T=tone (whole step), S=semitone (half step))

You should already know the scales of C, D, G and F major which are covered in Grade One Music Theory.

In Grade Two there are three new major scales which you need to know: **A, Bb** and **Eb** major.

### A MAJOR SCALE

A major has three sharps - F#, C# and G#. Here's the scale of A major ascending (going up) and descending (going down) in the treble and bass clefs:

### B FLAT AND E FLAT MAJOR SCALES

Bb major has two flats - Bb and Eb. Here's Bb major in full:

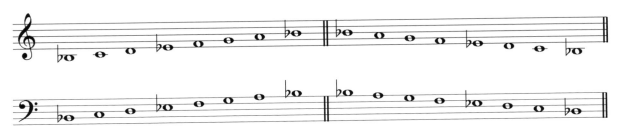

Eb major has three flats - Bb, Eb and Ab. Here's Eb major:

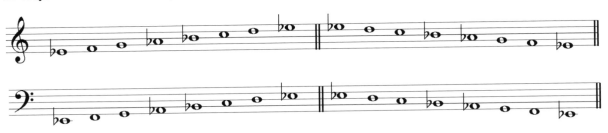

Tip! All major keys which have the word "flat" in their name have flats in the scale but no sharps, and all keys with the word "sharp" in their name contain sharps but no flats!

That's another reason why we always write Eb in the scale of Bb major, and never D#, for example.

Remember, in a scale, you can use each **letter name only once**, except for the first and last note.

## 3. MAJOR SCALES EXERCISES

### EXERCISE 1

What is the pattern of tones (whole steps) and semitones (half steps) in major scales?

### EXERCISE 2

Name the key of each of these major scales, and say whether it is **ascending** or **descending**.

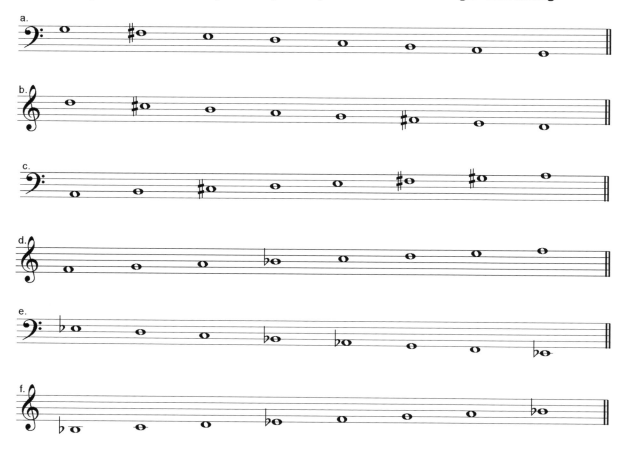

### EXERCISE 3

Complete these major scales, (which all start on the tonic), by adding the missing notes in the places marked *.

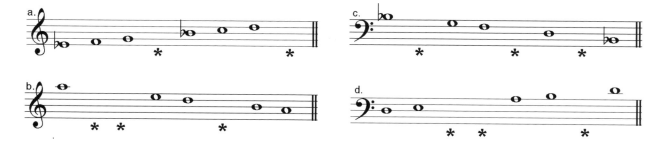

## 3. MAJOR SCALES ANSWERS

### EXERCISE 1

T – T – S – T – T – T – S

(or W – W – H – W – W – W – H)

### EXERCISE 2

a. G major descending

b. D major descending

c. A major ascending

d. F major ascending

e. Eb major descending

f. Bb major ascending

### EXERCISE 3

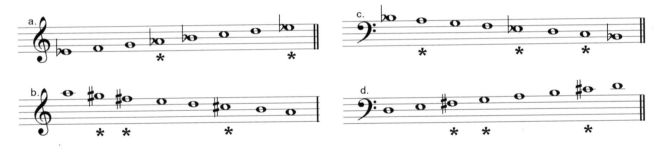

# 4. MINOR SCALES

**Minor scales** sound different to major scales because they are built on a different pattern of tones (whole steps) and semitones (half steps).

Many people think that minor scales sound sad, compared to major scales, which sound happy.

## TYPES OF MINOR SCALES

Although there is only one kind of major scale, there are three kinds of minor scale - **"harmonic"**, **"melodic"** and **"natural"**.

For the ABRSM Grade Two Online Music Theory exam (from July 2020), you will only be asked about harmonic minor. You will not be asked about the natural or melodic minor scale. If you are sitting the paper-based exam, you will be asked to choose between harmonic and melodic minor scales. For the Trinity Grade Two Music Theory exam, you need to know the harmonic and natural minor scales. We think it's a good idea to learn about all three kinds while you're studying, so let's find out what the difference is!

## HARMONIC MINOR SCALES - A, E AND D.

Harmonic minor scales are built on this pattern:

T - S - T - T - S - 3S - S

T=Tone (or "whole step") - S=Semitone (or "half step") - "3S" = three semitones

Let's start by building a scale of A minor harmonic ascending (going up):

And now let's look at A minor harmonic descending (going down):

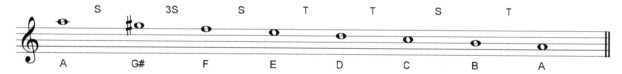

As you can see, it's exactly the same notes, but in reverse order.

Let's look at the two other minor scales you need to know for Grade Two Music Theory, E minor and D minor.

Play them slowly on a piano, and look carefully at how many semitones there are between each note.

## MINOR MELODIC SCALES

**Melodic** minor scales are a bit more complicated, because they have one pattern on the way up, but another on the way down.

On the way up (ascending), the pattern is T - S - T - T- **T - T - S**

but on the way down the pattern is **T - T - S** - T - T - S - T

As you can see, the descending scale is not just a back-to-front ascending scale, (as it was in the harmonic minor scales, and in the major scales).

The top end of the melodic scale uses a **completely different** pattern. The very top note will always be the tonic (keynote) of the scale, but the two notes just below it are the ones which change, depending on which direction you're going in.

Here's A minor melodic, ascending and descending. The notes in the boxes are the ones which change in the descending scale.

Let's see how E minor melodic and D minor melodic look:

E Minor Melodic:

D Minor Melodic:

## SCALES AND KEY SIGNATURES

We'll learn about the key signatures for these scales in Lesson 7 - Key Signatures, and Lesson 8 - Writing Scales.

## EXTRA INFO

Just in case you were wondering, in music theory the words "harmonic" and "melodic" can be used to describe **intervals** as well as scales- but when we use them to talk about intervals they have a different meaning. You'll learn about harmonic and melodic intervals in Lesson 14 - Intervals.

It's correct to say "melodic minor scale" and "minor melodic scale". It doesn't matter which way round! The same goes for harmonic scales.

# 4. MINOR SCALES EXERCISES

## EXERCISE 1

Name each of these minor scales and say whether it is **ascending** or **descending**.

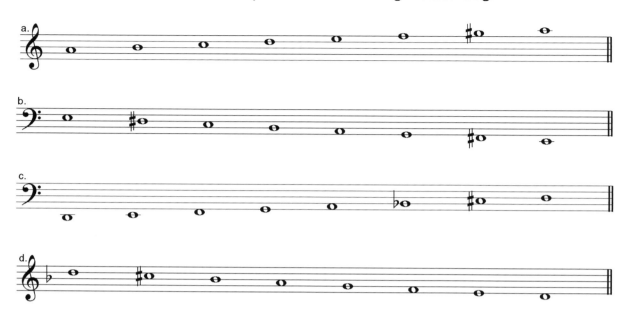

## EXERCISE 2

Add the missing notes to these minor scales.

### a. D minor harmonic

### b. A minor harmonic

### c. E minor harmonic

# 4. MINOR SCALES ANSWERS

## EXERCISE 1

a. A minor harmonic ascending

b. E minor harmonic descending

c. D minor harmonic ascending

d. D minor harmonic descending

## EXERCISE 2

a.

b.

c.

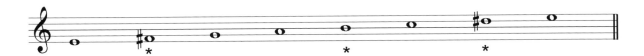

# 5. DEGREES OF THE SCALE

## WHAT ARE THE DEGREES OF THE SCALE?

Any note of any scale can be given a **number** as well as a name. The first/last note of the scale is often called the "tonic" or "keynote". In the key of C major, C is the tonic. It's also known as the "first degree of the scale", because it is the first note.

## DEGREES OF THE C MAJOR SCALE

Here's a scale of C major ascending, with all the **degrees of the scale** added:

D is the 2nd degree of the scale, E is the third, and so on.

It's important to remember that we work out the degrees of the scale from the **ascending** (upwards) scale only. If we write out the descending scale, we will need to reverse the order of the numbers:

## DEGREES OF MINOR MELODIC SCALES

As we learnt in Lesson 4 - Minor Scales, minor melodic scales are **different** on the way down. So what happens to the degrees of the scale? Let's take a look.

We'll look more closely at one of our new scales, E minor melodic. First we'll write out the ascending scale, then add the degrees of the scale under each note:

Look at the top end of the scale: C# is the 6th and D# is the 7th degree of the scale.

Now we'll write out the descending form of E melodic minor, and add in the numbers:

In E minor melodic descending, there is no D#, only D natural, and no C#, only C natural. This doesn't make any difference to the **degree** of the scale. So, we can say that the 6th degree of the scale of E minor melodic is C natural *or* C sharp.

## WORKING OUT THE DEGREE OF THE SCALE

To work out what degree of the scale a note is on, all you need to do is count **upwards** from the first note (or "tonic" or "keynote") of the scale.

Here are two questions for you:

1) What degree of the scale of Bb major is this note? In Bb major, the tonic is Bb. The second note is C, and the third note is D. This note is D (notice the bass clef!), so it's the **third degree of the scale of Bb major**.

2) What note is the 5th degree of the scale of A minor?
In A minor, A is the first note. B=2, C=3, D=4 and E=5. So **E** is the 5th degree of the scale of A minor.

## 5. DEGREES OF THE SCALE EXERCISES

### EXERCISE 1

Name the degree of the scale (e.g. 1st , 2nd) of each of the notes marked *.

a. The key is E minor

b. The key is G major

c. The key is D minor

d. The key is A major

### EXERCISE 2

a.  The key is Eb major. What is the 6th degree of the scale?

b.  The key is A minor. What is the 7th degree of the scale?

c.  The key is Bb major. What is the 4th degree of the scale?

### EXERCISE 3

a.  The key is D minor. What degree of the scale is Bb?

b.  The key is F major. What degree of the scale is E?

c.  The key is A major. What degree of the scale is C#?

## 5. DEGREES OF THE SCALE ANSWERS

### EXERCISE 1

a.

1st     5th     3rd     2nd  7th  etc.

b.

5th  3rd  1st 7th  6th  etc.

c.

1st  6th  5th  3rd  7th  etc.

d.

5th  4th  3rd  1st  6th  etc.

### EXERCISE 2

a.  C

b.  G#

c.  Eb

### EXERCISE 3

a.  6th

b.  7th

c.  3rd

# 6. KEY SIGNATURES AND ACCIDENTALS

## KEYS AND KEY SIGNATURES

If a melody uses mostly the notes of the Bb major scale, we say that the music is "in the key of" Bb major.

We don't write out the flat symbols for the Bs and the Es every time they appear in the music - because there would probably be rather a lot of them!

Instead, we use a **key signature**: at the beginning of each new line of music, we write a Bb and an Eb, to remind us that **all** the Bs and **all** the Es need to be flattened.

The key signature also tells us very quickly that the music is in Bb major, without having to count all the flats!

Here's a key signature of Bb major, with the note names marked under the melody:

## ACCIDENTALS

Sometimes we need to add extra flats, sharps and naturals within a melody, even when we have already got a key signature.

It might be because

- the music changes key for a short time, or

- just because they sound nice, or

- because the music is in a **minor** key.

If we add sharps, flats and naturals inside the music itself, they are called "accidentals". Special rules apply to all accidentals.

## POSITION OF ACCIDENTALS

Accidentals are always written on the **left** side of the note they affect.

Also make sure that the symbol is written on the same space/line as the note it applies to.

## RULES FOR ACCIDENTALS

Accidentals don't only affect the note they are written next to. After an accidental has been written, every other note of the **same position** on the stave is also affected, but **only until the next bar line**.

(Unlike key signatures, accidentals only affect the other notes at the **same position on the stave.** Sharps and flats in key signatures affect all the notes with the same letter name, whatever their position on the stave.)

- Note 1 is C natural
- Note 2 is C sharp, because of the accidental
- Note 3 is also C sharp, because it's in the same bar
- Note 4 is C natural, because the sharp is "cancelled" (stopped) by the bar line

When a note is tied across a bar line, any accidental will also apply to the note in the **next** bar as well, even if there is no accidental.

- Note 1 is Bb because of the key signature
- Note 2 is B natural because of the accidental
- Note 3 is also B natural, because it's tied to the previous B natural

## KEY SIGNATURES WITH ACCIDENTALS

Now let's see what happens when we have both a key signature and accidentals together.

Here's a couple of bars of music in the key of Bb major, so the key signature has two flats, Bb and Eb:

- Note 1 is Bb, because of the key signature
- Note 2 is B natural, because of the accidental
- Note 3 is also B natural, because it's in the same bar as note 2
- Note 4 is B flat, because the barline cancels (stops) the natural accidental

Now you are confident working with both key signatures and accidentals, in the next lesson we'll move on to the types of question you might get in the Grade Two Music Theory exam which involve using them.

# 6. KEY SIGNATURES AND ACCIDENTALS EXERCISES

## EXERCISE 1

Answer true or false to the following statements:

a. If a B flat is written in a key signature, it applies to all the B's in the piece.

b. If a B flat is written as an accidental, it applies to all the B's in that bar.

c. If a Bb with an accidental is tied across a bar line to another Bb, the second Bb will also need a flat symbol as an accidental.

## EXERCISE 2

Give the letter name of each of the notes marked *, including the sharp or flat sign where necessary.

a.

b.

c.

d.

## 6. KEY SIGNATURES AND ACCIDENTALS ANSWERS

### EXERCISE 1

a. True

b. False. It only applies to notes of the exact same pitch, and it only applies to notes written **after** the accidental (and not before it).

c. False. The accidental is included in the tie and does not need to be written again.

### EXERCISE 2

a.

b.

c.

d.

# 7. WORKING WITH KEY SIGNATURES

## MAJOR KEY SIGNATURES WITH SHARPS

The major scales that we've learned which use sharp key signatures are G, D and A major. The sharps in key signatures are always written in this order:

F# - C# - G#

in these treble clef positions:

G major    D major    A major

and these bass clef positions:

G major    D major    A major

You need to learn the **exact** positions of the sharps on the staff.

incorrect position

The F sharp and G sharp need to be moved up an octave. Remember that the F# is always the one highest on the stave, and then the pattern goes "down and up".

## MAJOR KEY SIGNATURES WITH FLATS

The major keys with flats we need to know about for Grade Two Music Theory are F, Bb and Eb. The flats are always written in this order:

Bb - Eb - Ab

The treble clef flats are always written in these positions:

Fmajor    Bb major    Eb major

and the bass clef flats are written in these positions:

Fmajor    Bb major    Eb major

Again, the **exact** position of the flats is important, so make sure you know where they go! The flats have an "up-down" pattern.

Music which is written in a minor key will usually use a mixture of a **key signature** plus **accidentals**.

There are no special **minor** key signatures in music theory - we use the same ones as in the major keys, but we write accidentals in the music where they are needed.

Let's look at A minor again, as an example. For grade 2, you need to know these 3 different A minor scales:

- A minor **harmonic**: A - B - C - D - E - F - G# - A

- A minor **melodic, ascending**: A - B - C - D - E - F# - G# - A

- A minor **melodic, descending**:  A - G - F - E - D - C - B - A

So, in our music, sometimes we might need F# or G# and sometimes not!

For the key signature, we use the notes in the **melodic minor descending scale**. For A minor, this means no sharps or flats, so it's the same key signature as C major.

The key signature for a minor key is always the same as the key signature for the major key which is the **3rd degree** of the minor scale.

Count up three notes from the tonic to find the key with the same key signature.

For example, in A minor, the 3rd degree of the scale is C, so A minor and C major have the same key signatures.

We use the words "**relative minor**" and "**relative major**" to talk about this relationship. For example, C major is the **relative major** to A minor.

In the Grade Two Music Theory exam, you also need to know about D minor and E minor, so let's work out the relative major keys for these two:

- D minor begins: D - E - F.
  F is the 3rd degree of the scale of D minor, so the key signature for D minor is the same as for F major - one flat.

- E minor begins: E - F# - G.
  G is the 3rd degree of the scale of E minor, so the key signature for E minor is the same as for G major - one sharp.

## RE-WRITING MUSIC WITH OR WITHOUT A KEY SIGNATURE

In the Grade Two Music Theory exam, you might be asked to copy out a short tune **with** or **without** a key signature.

If the melody has already got a key signature, you'll have to write it **without**, and if it doesn't have a key signature, you'll have to re-write the music **with** a key signature.

### FROM "WITH" A KEY SIGNATURE TO "WITHOUT"

Look carefully at the key signature and accidentals in this melody, and think about which notes need to have sharps or flats next to them:

**All** the Bs and Es will need to be flat, the low ones and the high ones, **except** where there are accidentals.

Start by pencilling in a cross above each flattened note, so you don't forget any.

Copy out the music **neatly**, adding the flats (or sharps) where they are needed.

Remember that you only need to put **one** accidental in a bar for it to affect the rest of the notes in that bar that are the same pitch.

Check whether you need to keep any of the accidentals from the original tune, like the E natural here.

Write the accidentals on the left side of the note, making sure they are right next to the note-head on the same line or space:

incorrect position

Here's the finished answer:

31

If you have to rewrite a melody **with** a key signature in your music theory exam, you will be told the key of the melody.

Start by putting in the correct **key signature**. Check above if you've forgotten how to write key signatures!

Now start to copy the notes.

Every time you come across an accidental, check if it's already in the key signature. If it is, don't copy it. If it isn't in the key signature, you'll need to keep it there in the music as an accidental.

We'll use the same tune as before, but work backwards on it!

The key is Bb major, so the key signature will have Bb and Eb in it.

The only accidental in this tune which is neither a Bb nor an Eb is the **E natural** in bar 4. So, we need to get rid of all the flats but keep this E natural:

Always go back and check your answers, as it's very easy to miss out an accidental by mistake!

# 7. WORKING WITH KEY SIGNATURES EXERCISES

## Exercise 1

Rewrite the following melodies, without using a key signature. Remember to include sharp, flat or natural signs where they are needed. The key and the first three notes are given in each melody.

### a. D minor

### b. Bb major

### c. F major

## Exercise 2

Rewrite the following melodies using the correct key signature. Leave out any unnecessary accidentals, but remember to include any that may be needed. The key and the first three notes are given for each melody.

### a. A major

### b. Eb major

### c. E minor

EXERCISE 1

EXERCISE 2

# 8. WRITING SCALES

## TYPES OF SCALES QUESTIONS

In the ABRSM Grade Two Music Theory exam there are lots of different types of questions with scales.

Here are some things you might have to do:

- Write a major or minor scale either ascending or descending, and either with or without a key signature.

- Add clefs, key signatures or accidentals to a given scale.

You will need to remember the pattern of tones and semitones (whole and half steps) for scales:

- For major scales the pattern is T-T-S-T-T-T-S.

- For minor harmonic scales, the pattern is T-S-T-T-S-3S-S.

- For minor melodic ascending scales, the pattern is T-S-T-T-T-T-S

- For minor melodic descending scales, the pattern is T-T-S-T-T-S-T

You will also need to remember the key signatures for the keys in this grade:

- C major/ A minor - no key signature

- G major / E minor - 1 sharp (F#)

- D major - 2 sharps (F#, C#)

- A major - 3 sharps (F#, C#, G#)

- F major / D minor - 1 flat (Bb)

- Bb major - 2 flats (Bb, Eb)

- Eb major - 3 flats (Bb, Eb, Ab)

More information about tones and semitones and about key signatures in previous lessons.

If you can't remember all the different patterns of tones and semitones, just learn the scales of C major and A minor (all types). Then use some scrap paper to write out those scales, and use them as a **template** to work out where the tones and semitones fall in the other scales.

The pattern of sharps goes up in 5ths: F#-C#-G#.

The pattern of flats goes up in 4ths: Bb-Eb-Ab

We now need to practice each type of question which might come up in the exam.

Here are four important rules for you:

1.  Read the question carefully and underline the keywords e.g. DESCENDING or WITH a KEY SIGNATURE.

2.  Write eight notes in total.

3.  Write ONE note per line or space.

4.  Use semibreves (whole notes).

Here's an example question, and the steps to follow to get full marks in your music theory exam:

*Write as semibreves (whole notes) the scale of A minor ascending, without a key signature but adding any necessary sharp or flat signs. State which form of the minor scale you have used.*

1.  Whatever the scale is, the first thing you need to do is put in your starting note (the tonic, or "keynote"). If you're writing an ascending scale, start low. For descending scales, start high. Make sure you leave enough room on the left for the key signature, if you need one.

2.  Next, using semibreves (whole notes), fill up the lines and spaces - one note per line/space, until you have **eight** notes. Don't draw the notes too close together!

3.  Look again at the **type** of scale you need to write - is it major or minor? Think about the sharps and flats you'll need for that scale - what sharps or flats appear in the **key signature**?

4.  Do you need to add any **extra accidentals**? Major scales and minor melodic descending scales don't need **any** extra accidentals. In minor harmonic scales you need to raise ONE note by a semitone (half step): the 7th degree of the scale. In minor melodic **ascending** scales you need to raise TWO notes by a semitone: the 6th and 7th degrees of the scale.

5.  Put in the key signature, if you've been asked to write one. Now add any necessary extra accidentals. (Note - you'll NEVER write a **flat** as an accidental in a scale with a key signature - only sharps and naturals are possible). If there is a key signature, remember that the only degrees of the scale which could ever need an accidental are the 7th (all minor scales) or 6th (melodic minor ascending).

6.  If you were asked to write the scale **without** a key signature, add the necessary sharps and flats next to each note of the scale. Don't forget to add an accidental to the top note of the scale if you are writing Bb or Eb major.

Let's work together through the scales question at the beginning of this lesson, using the steps we suggested above.

1) We write the first note: A. It's an **ascending** scale, so we start with an A low on the stave:

2) We'll fill up the lines and spaces, until we have 8 notes:

3) We need to write a minor scale, without a key signature. (We'll choose A minor **harmonic**.) A minor has no sharps or flats in the key signature, like its relative major, C major.

4 & 5) Minor harmonic scales have a raised 7th degree of the scale, so we need a G sharp. Let's put it in.

That's our finished scale of A minor (harmonic) ascending.


## ADDING CLEFS & KEY SIGNATURES

Sometimes you'll be asked to write in the **clef** and/or key signature of a scale.

Look at the first note and key of the scale. Decide if the first note must be treble or bass clef:

G major

In this scale, the first note needs to be a G, so we should write a treble clef. The key of G major has one sharp: F#. Add the clef, then the key signature.

G major

# 8. WRITING SCALES EXERCISES

## EXERCISE 1

Add the correct clef and any necessary sharp or flat signs to make each of the scales named below. Do not use a key signature.

a. E flat major

b. G major

c. A major

d. D minor. Which form of the minor scale have you used?

## EXERCISE 2

Write as semibreves (whole notes) the scales named below, with the key signature.

a. F major ascending

b. Bb major descending

c. D major ascending

d. A minor descending. Which form of the scale have you used?

## Exercise 3

Write as semibreves (whole notes) the scales named below, without a key signature but adding any necessary sharp or flat signs.

a. D major descending

b. Bb major ascending

c. E minor descending. Which form of the scale have you used?

d. E flat major descending

# 8. WRITING SCALES ANSWERS

## EXERCISE 1

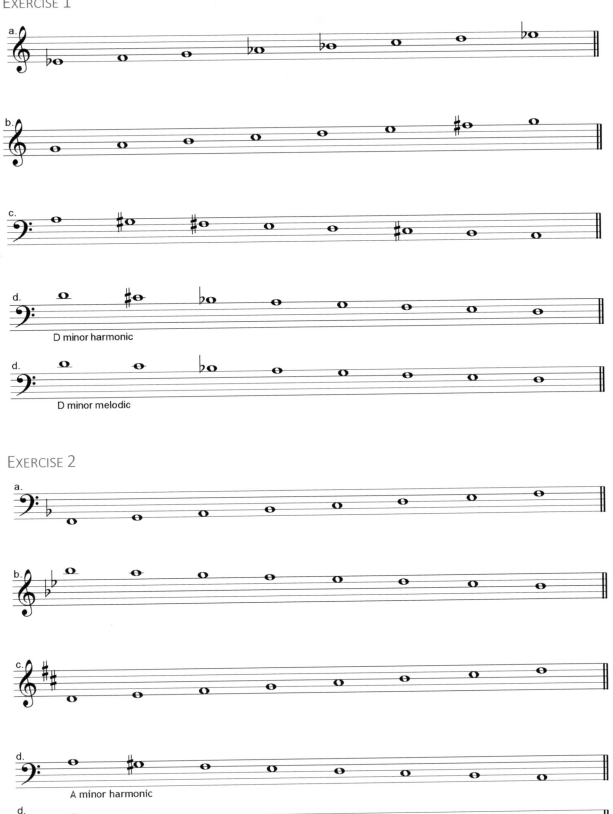

d. D minor harmonic

d. D minor melodic

## EXERCISE 2

a.

b.

c.

d. A minor harmonic

d. A minor melodic

a.
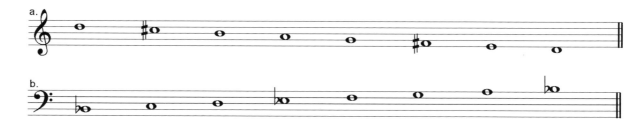

b.

c. E minor harmonic

c. E minor melodic
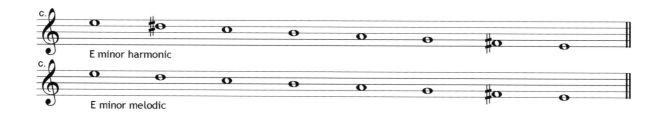

d.

# 9. SIMPLE TIME SIGNATURES (UK)

## QUICK TIME SIGNATURES REVIEW

In Grade One Music Theory we learned three time signatures: 2/4, 3/4 and 4/4. We learned that the lower number "4" tells us that we need to count crotchet beats and that the top number tells us **how many** beats to count.

So, 2/4 means "count 2 crotchets per bar", 3/4 means "count 3 crotchets per bar" and 4/4 means "count 4 crotchets per bar".

## NEW FOR GRADE TWO MUSIC THEORY

In Grade Two Music Theory, we have some new time signatures to look at.

First, let's look at 2/2, 3/2 and 4/2.

The lower number "2" tells us to count minims. 2/2 means "count two minims per bar", 3/2 means "count three minims per bar" and 4/2 means "count four minims per bar".

And finally, we need to know 3/8. The lower number 8 tells us to count quavers, so 3/8 means "count three quavers per bar".

All the time signatures you have learned so far (3/8, 2/4, 3/4, 4/4, 2/2, 3/2 and 4/2) are **simple** time signatures. All simple time signatures have 2, 3 or 4 as their top number.

## TYPES OF QUESTION

In the Grade Two Music Theory exam, you might get a question asking you something like this:

*Complete this sentence:*
*The time signature 2/4 means that there are two ........... beats in a bar.*

We need to figure out what kind of beats - so we look at the lower number. The lower number is "4", which means "crotchet" beats. So, the correct answer is "The time signature 2/4 means that there are two **crotchet** beats in a bar".

## WRITING TIME SIGNATURES

In a typed page like this one, it's ok to write out time signatures as two numbers with a slash between them, like so - 3/8. But when you write time signatures on a stave, in your music theory exam you should make sure you don't write them like this! On a stave, time signatures should be written **one number directly above the other** and **without** a slash or line, like so:

$$\frac{3}{4}$$

Time signatures are placed at the beginning of the stave, after the clef and key signature. They only appear right at the beginning of a piece (unless there is a change of time signature in the middle of the piece somewhere).

Here are some short tunes using the new time signatures from the grade two music theory syllabus. Play them through on your instrument.

2/2 – Two minim beats per bar

This time signature is almost exactly the same as 4/4. They both have the same total number of notes per bar. The difference is that in 2/2, the note which falls on the second minim beat of the bar is accented slightly more heavily than it would be in 4/4. Most people can't tell the difference just by listening though!

3/2 – Three minim beats per bar

This time signature has three beats per bar, just like the time signature of 3/4. The difference is that in 3/2, the notes used for each beat are twice as long. Instead of three crotchets, you would find three minims. The last note in this example is a dotted semibreve, which is worth the same as six crotchets.

4/2 – Four minim beats per bar

This time signature isn't very common, but you may come across it, particularly in very old pieces. It is just like 4/4, but each beat is twice as long.

3/8 – Three quaver beats per bar

This time signature is normally used in a quick tempo and has a dance-like feel to it. Although there are three beats per bar, often it just feels like one beat per bar, as it skips along.

# 9. SIMPLE TIME SIGNATURES (USA)

## QUICK TIME SIGNATURES REVIEW

In Grade One Music Theory we learned three time signatures: 2/4, 3/4 and 4/4. We learned that the lower number "4" tells us that we need to count quarter note beats and that the top number tells us **how many** beats to count.

So, 2/4 means "count 2 quarter notes per measure", 3/4 means "count 3 quarter notes per measure" and 4/4 means "count 4 quarter notes per measure".

## NEW FOR GRADE TWO MUSIC THEORY

In Grade Two Music Theory, we have some new time signatures to look at.

First, let's look at 2/2, 3/2 and 4/2.

The lower number "2" tells us to count half notes. 2/2 means "count two half notes per measure", 3/2 means "count three half notes per measure" and 4/2 means "count four half notes per measure".

And finally, we need to know 3/8. The lower number 8 tells us to count eighth notes, so 3/8 means "count three eighth notes per measure".

All the time signatures you have learned so far (3/8, 2/4, 3/4, 4/4, 2/2, 3/2 and 4/2) are **simple** time signatures. All simple time signatures have 2, 3 or 4 as their top number.

## TYPES OF QUESTION

In the Grade Two Music Theory exam, you might get a question asking you something like this:

*Complete this sentence:*
*The time signature 2/4 means that there are two ........... beats in a bar.*

"Bar" is the UK word for "measure". We need to figure out what kind of beats - so we look at the lower number. The lower number is "4", which means "quarter note" beats. So, the correct answer is "The time signature 2/4 means that there are two **quarter note** beats in a bar".

## WRITING TIME SIGNATURES

In a typed page like this one, it's ok to write out time signatures as two numbers with a slash between them, like so - 3/8. But when you write time signatures on a staff, in your music theory exam you should make sure you don't write them like this! On a staff, time signatures should be written **one number directly above the other** and **without** a slash or line, like so:

Time signatures are placed at the beginning of the staff, after the clef and key signature. They only appear right at the beginning of a piece (unless there is a change of time signature in the middle of the piece somewhere).

Here are some short tunes using the new time signatures from the grade two music theory syllabus. Play them through on your instrument.

## 2/2 – Two half note beats per bar

This time signature is almost exactly the same as 4/4. They both have the same total number of notes per bar. The difference is that in 2/2, the note which falls on the second half note beat of the bar is accented slightly more heavily than it would be in 4/4. Most people can't tell the difference just by listening though!

## 3/2 – Three half note beats per bar

This time signature has three beats per bar, just like the time signature of 3/4. The difference is that in 3/2, the notes used for each beat are twice as long. Instead of three quarter notes, you would find three half notes. The last note in this example is a dotted whole note, which is worth the same as six quarter notes.

## 4/2 – Four half note beats per bar

This time signature isn't very common, but you may come across it, particularly in very old pieces. It is just like 4/4, but each beat is twice as long.

## 3/8 – Three eighth note beats per bar

This time signature is normally used in a quick tempo and has a dance-like feel to it. Although there are three beats per bar, often it just feels like one beat per bar, as it skips along.

# 9. SIMPLE TIME SIGNATURES EXERCISES

## EXERCISE 1

True or False?

a.   The time signature $\frac{2}{4}$ means there are four crotchet (quarter note) beats per bar.

b.   The time signature $\frac{3}{2}$ means there are three minim (half note) beats per bar.

## EXERCISE 2

a.   The time signature $\frac{4}{4}$ means that there are four _____ beats in a bar.

b.   The time signature $\frac{2}{2}$ means that there are two _____ beats in a bar.

## EXERCISE 3

a.   Which time signature means there are three quaver (eighth note) beats per bar?

b.   Which time signature means there are two minim (half note) beats per bar?

c.   Which time signature means there are three crotchet (quarter note) beats per bar?

## EXERCISE 4

Which of these staves shows the correct order of symbols?

# 9. SIMPLE TIME SIGNATURES ANSWERS

## EXERCISE 1

a. False
b. True

## EXERCISE 2

a. The time signature $\frac{4}{4}$ means that there are four <u>crotchet (quarter note)</u> beats in a bar.

b. The time signature $\frac{2}{2}$ means that there are two <u>minim (half note)</u> beats in a bar.

## EXERCISE 3

d. 3/8

e. 2/2

f. 3/4

## EXERCISE 4

The correct stave is b.

# 10. WORKING WITH TIME SIGNATURES

In the Grade Two Music Theory exam, your knowledge of time signatures will be tested in a variety of ways. Here are some of the questions that are likely to come up:

- Adding bar lines to a melody with a given time signature

- Adding a time signature to a melody with given bar lines

- Rewriting a melody in a new time signature

- Adding rests of the correct time value

- Composing a rhythm

- Questions about the meaning of the numbers in time signatures

In this lesson we will look at adding bar lines or a time signature. Rewriting in a new time signature is explained in lesson 11, adding rests in lesson 12, and composing a rhythm is covered in lesson 16.

## ADDING BAR LINES

If you are asked to add bar lines to a short melody, you'll be given the time signature and the first bar line will be in place already.

The question could look something like this:

*Add the missing bar lines to this tune. The first bar line is given.*

Look carefully at the time signature - **how many** beats are there per bar, and **what type** of beats are they?

This melody is in 3/4, so we need to have three crotchet (quarter note) beats per bar.

Underneath each note, carefully pencil in its value, like this:

Now count out the note values, and draw a bar line when each bar has the value of three crotchets (quarter notes):

See lesson 15 for more about adding bar lines to melodies that contain triplets.

## How to Draw Bar Lines in Your Music Theory Exam

You could lose points if your work is messy or difficult to read. Always use a ruler to draw your bar lines neatly. Place them closer to the edge of the **1st** note in the bar, like this:

Don't draw the bar line too close the **last** note of the bar, and make sure you leave more space for longer note values. This bar line is in the wrong place because there isn't enough space after the minim (half note), and it's not close enough to the crotchet (quarter note):

This bar line is also in the wrong place, because it's more or less exactly half way between the two notes, instead of being closer to the crotchet (quarter note):

In the Grade Two Theory Exam, every bar should normally be a complete bar, even the last one (although in real life the last bar can be incomplete).

## Working Out a Time Signature

The method for adding a time signature is the opposite of that for adding bar lines.

Here's an example question:

*Add the time signature to this tune.*

Start by counting the notes in each bar. Use a value of 1 for a crotchet (quarter note), 1/2 for a quaver (eighth note), 2 for a minim (half note) and so on. Group quavers (8th notes) and semiquavers (16th notes) together to make complete beats:

Here you can see that each bar contains **three** crotchet (quarter note) beats. The top number of the time signature tells you **how many** beats to count in each bar, so the top number must be 3 in this case. The lower number tells you **what kind** of beats to count, and the number 4 means "crotchet" (quarter note) beats, so our time signature needs to be 3/4.

Remember that the **lower** number of the time signature tells you the **type** of beats you need to count. In Grade Two, there are only three possibilities:

- 2 = minims (half notes)

- 4 = crotchets (quarter notes)

- 8 = quavers (eighth notes)

And, in Grade Two, there are only three possibilities for the top number too. Your top number will always be 2, 3 or 4. This means the answer can only be one of these time signatures: 3/8, 2/4, 3/4, 4/4, 2/2, 3/2 or 4/2.

Let's try another question, this time a bit harder. What's the time signature for this tune?

When you count up the notes in each bar, you'll find there are in fact 8 crotchet (quarter note) beats per bar. So is the time signature 8/4?

Well, no. (The time signature 8/4 *does* exist, but it's very rare and it's definitely **not** on the Grade Two Music Theory syllabus!)

We can count the minims (half notes) instead, and we'll find that we have four minim beats per bar.

When we count minims (half notes), the time signature has the number "2" as the bottom number. We counted four minims, so the time signature must be 4/2. Other "minim" (half note) time signatures you might see in the Grade Two music theory exam are 2/2 and 3/2.

Here's a final question. What time signature do we need here?

Here, we can't count crotchets (quarter notes), because we would have one and a half beats per bar, which is not possible - no half beats allowed! We can't count minims (half notes) either, so we'll need to count quavers (eighth notes).

This melody has three quaver (8th note) beats in each bar, so the time signature must be 3/8. Remember that the "8" means "quaver beats" (eighth note beats).

## 2/2 OR 4/4?

You might be wondering what the difference is between 4/4 and 2/2, as they have exactly the same number of beats per bar?

Well, the answer is, not much! If you see lots of minims (half notes), you could choose the 2/2 time signature. If you see lots of crotchets (quarter notes), you could use the 4/4 time signature. But don't worry if you're not sure which one it should be - in the Grade Two music theory exam these two time signatures are completely interchangeable.

Here are some typical 4/4 bars - you can usually find crotchets and quavers (quarters and eighths) in the melody:

## 10. WORKING WITH TIME SIGNATURES EXERCISES
### EXERCISE 1

Add the missing bar lines to these tunes. The first bar line is given in each.

a.

b.

c.

d.

### EXERCISE 2

Add the time signature to each of these tunes.

a.

b.

c.

d.

# 10. WORKING WITH TIME SIGNATURES ANSWERS

## EXERCISE 1

a.

b.

c.

d.

## EXERCISE 2

a.  2/4

b.  4/2

c.  3/8

d.  3/2

# 11. REWRITING IN A NEW TIME SIGNATURE

## WHAT'S NEW IN GRADE TWO

Grade 2 Music Theory introduces a new kind of exercise with time signatures which you didn't see in Grade 1: rewriting music in a **new** time signature.

The question will ask you to rewrite a melody using notes and rests which have either **TWICE** or **HALF** the value of the original.

The new time signature will already be in place, and you'll get a few notes done for you to get you started.

## TWICE THE VALUE

Here's an example question:

*Rewrite the following in notes of twice the value, beginning as shown.*

There's actually nothing very complicated about doing this!

Start by jotting down, lightly in pencil, the value of each note in order, like this:

Each of the original notes needs to be **twice** as long. This means you need to change each one into the next longest type of note. So, if you have a

## DEALING WITH DOTTED NOTES AND TIES

What do we do with dotted notes? Just change them in the same way, but keep the dot there!

Looking at small dotted notes like quavers (eighth notes) can get confusing, so let's compare a dotted crotchet and a dotted minim to see what happens.

𝅝. = 3 crotchets (quarter notes)

♩. = 1.5 crotchets (quarter notes)

So, you can see that a dotted minim (half note) is **twice as long** as a dotted crotchet (quarter note). In the same way, a dotted quaver (eighth note) is twice as long as a dotted semiquaver (16th note), and so on.

Here's the finished answer to our question:

Tied notes don't need any special treatment either - just add any ties in the same place in your rewritten tune.


## HALF THE VALUE

If you are asked to rewrite the music in notes/rests of **half** the value, the process is the same, but the other way round.

A semibreve (whole note) will become a minim (half note), a minim will become a crotchet (quarter note) and so on.

Again, dots don't make a difference, just keep them there! Look at the finished answer for the question we just did - if we **halve** all the note values in our answer we'll get back to the original note values again!

Make sure you write your notes and rests out as neatly as you can, and don't forget to add any ties or accidentals if necessary!

## 11. REWRITING IN A NEW TIME SIGNATURE EXERCISES
### EXERCISE 1

Rewrite the following tunes in notes and rests of **half** the value, beginning as shown.

### EXERCISE 2

Rewrite the following tunes in notes and rests of **twice** the value, beginning as shown.

## 11. REWRITING IN A NEW TIME SIGNATURE ANSWERS

### EXERCISE 1

### EXERCISE 2

# 12. ADDING RESTS

## RESTS REVIEW

Do you remember how to draw each of the rests correctly?

Here's some quick revision. The names in British English are:

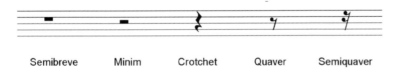

| Semibreve | Minim | Crotchet | Quaver | Semiquaver |

And in American English:

| Whole | Half | Quarter | Eighth | Sixteenth |

## HOW TO ADD RESTS TO A MELODY

If you get a question asking you to add a rest or rest to a melody, the first thing you need to check is the time signature.

Here's an example question:

*Add the correct rest(s) at the places marked * in this tune to make each bar complete.*

The time signature is 2/2, so we need to have 2 minim (half note) beats per bar.

Find the first bar with missing rests, and pencil in the values of the notes that you **do** have. Add small values together to make **complete beats**, where you can.

Here we can see that we only have one and a half beats in the second half of the bar, where in fact we need 2. So we need a quaver (eighth note) to complete the full minim beat.

Here's the rest added to the bar:

1 + 1
=
2

½ + ½ + ½
=
1½

Try to work out the other rests for yourself, in the same way. Remember that your rests need to make **complete beats**. Think carefully about the last bar - you need to complete the first minim (half note) beat first, then finish the bar off, so you'll need two rests in the last bar.

Here is the answer:

## IS THIS WRONG?

Look at that last bar again. Students often wonder if it's wrong to write something like a dotted minim (half) rest, or a minim followed by a crotchet (quarter), in this type of bar. After all, it's just a silence isn't it, so does it really matter?

Well, the short answer is, yes, it does matter! You **must** look carefully at the time signature, and you **must** make up **complete beats** before you do anything else.

Here's another example. In 4/4, there are four crotchet (quarter note) beats per bar. So how should you fill up a bar like this with rests?

So far the notes in the bar make up a total of 3 beats (1½ +½+½+½). Since we need four in total, you might be tempted to write a crotchet (quarter) rest here, but you'd be wrong. The rests you choose need to make it obvious to the eye where the beats of the bar fall. If you write a crotchet (quarter) rest, the position of beat 3 will be hidden – somewhere in the middle of that rest.

Instead, you need to write a quaver (eighth) rest first, to finish off the second beat, then another one to begin the third beat.

## 12. ADDING RESTS EXERCISES
### Exercise 1

In each of the numbered spaces add the rest named below, as shown in the answer to [1].

[1] crotchet (quarter) rest

[3] whole bar (whole measure) rest

[2] quaver (eighth) rest

[4] dotted crotchet (quarter) rest

[5] semibreve (whole) rest

[8] minim (half) rest

[6] semiquaver (sixteenth) rest

[9] crotchet (quarter) rest

[7] quaver (eighth) rest

[10] minim (half) rest

[12] quaver (eighth) rest

[11] semibreve (whole) rest

### Exercise 2

Add the correct rest(s) at the places marked * in these tunes, to make each bar complete.

## 12. ADDING RESTS ANSWERS

### EXERCISE 1

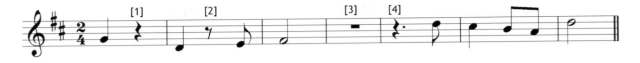

### EXERCISE 2

# 13. TONIC TRIADS

## Building Tonic Triads

What are tonic triads? Tonic triads are simple chords with just three notes in them. To build a tonic triad, we start by taking the **first** note from any scale (this note is also known as the "tonic" or "key note"). Let's make a tonic triad of D major.

We start by writing the first note of the scale of D major - D:

Next we add a note which is 2 notes higher (also known as the third degree of the scale). In the scale of D major, the note which is 2 notes higher than D is F#:

Finally, we add the note which is two notes higher than the last note - otherwise known as the fifth degree of the scale. In the scale of D major, the fifth degree of the scale is A:

The notes D-F#-A make up the tonic triad in the key of D major.

We can also build tonic triads in minor keys of course. The rules are the same, but we need to use the minor scale. In D minor, the tonic is D, the third degree of the scale is F (natural) and the fifth degree of the scale is A. So, the tonic triad of D minor looks like this:

Tonic triads are always built on the tonic, third and fifth degrees of the scale of the same key.

## Adding a Clef to a Tonic Triad

You might be asked to add a clef (either treble or bass) to a tonic triad. You'll see the tonic triad on the stave, and will be told what key it's in, like this:

G major

Remember that tonic triads are always built on the **first** note of the scale, so in this tonic triad, the lowest note has to be a G, because the key is G major. This note will be a G if we add a bass clef:

G major

## ADDING ACCIDENTALS TO A TONIC TRIAD

Sometimes you might need to add some accidentals as well as a clef. Look at this tonic triad:

Here we need to add a treble clef, so that the lowest note is a B, and we also need to put a flat sign on the B, to make it a Bb:

## NAMING THE KEY OF A TONIC TRIAD

Another type of question you might get in the Grade Two Theory Exam, is to **name the key** of a tonic triad. Again, you need to think first about the **lowest note** of the chord. Look carefully at the **clef** and the **key signature** or **accidentals** too. You should also look at the middle note of the chord to see if it's a **major** or a **minor** tonic triad.

*What key is this tonic triad in?*

The lowest note is A (it's in the bass clef), so it's a tonic triad in the key of A. The middle note is C#, which is the third degree of the scale in A major (in A minor, the third degree of the scale is C **natural**). So, this tonic triad is in **A major**.

## GRADE TWO TONIC TRIADS

Here's a list of all the tonic triads you'll need to recognise for Grade Two, in both the treble and bass clef:

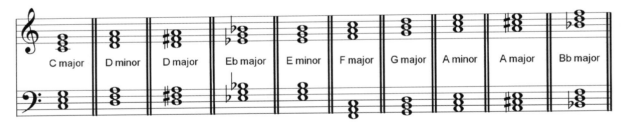

## FINDING TONIC TRIADS IN A MELODY

Sometimes you might need to find three notes in a melody which form a tonic triad when they're put together. You'll be told what key the melody is in, and could see a question like this:

*This melody is in C major. In which bar can all three notes of the tonic triad be found?*

Because the piece is in C major, the tonic triad must contain the notes C-E-G. (They could be in any order). Bar two contains the notes C, E and G, so that's the right answer. (Bar one doesn't contain a G, so it's not right!)

## 13. TONIC TRIADS EXERCISES

### EXERCISE 1

Add the correct clef and any necessary sharp or flat signs to each of these tonic triads. Do *not* use a key signature.

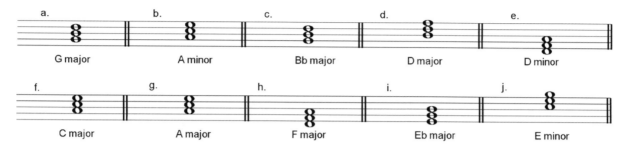

### EXERCISE 2

Name the keys of these tonic triads.

### EXERCISE 3

Draw a circle round 3 notes next to each other that form the tonic triad. (The key is given.)

Bb major

D major

### EXERCISE 4

In which bar can all three notes of the tonic triad be found? (The key is given.)

Eb major

A minor

## 13. TONIC TRIADS ANSWERS

### EXERCISE 1

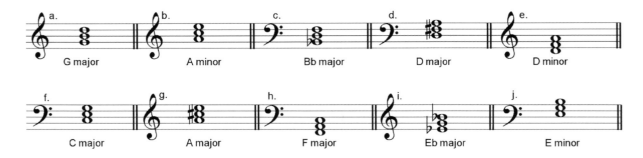

a. G major b. A minor c. Bb major d. D major e. D minor

f. C major g. A major h. F major i. Eb major j. E minor

### EXERCISE 2

a. A major
b. Bb major
c. G major

d. E minor
e. D major
f. A minor

### EXERCISE 3

### EXERCISE 4

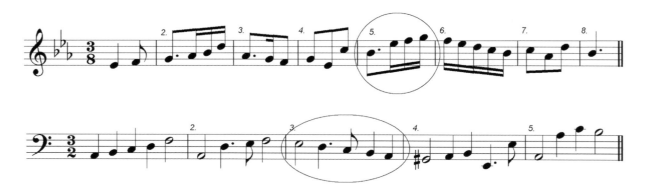

66

# 14. INTERVALS

## NEW FOR GRADE TWO

What you need to know about intervals for the Grade Two theory exam is more or less the same as for Grade One.

You need to be able to write and recognise any **harmonic** or **melodic** interval, written in any of the keys for this grade (C, D, Eb, F, G, A and Bb major and A, E and D minor).

There are no new techniques to learn, just the new keys.

## HARMONIC AND MELODIC INTERVALS

A **harmonic interval** is the distance between two notes played at the same time. It is called a "harmonic interval", because the two notes together create harmony, or a chord.

A **melodic interval** is the distance between two notes played one after the other. It's called a "melodic interval", because the two notes occur as part of a melody.

## WORKING OUT INTERVALS

The method of working out intervals is the same for both melodic and harmonic intervals: Count up the letter names, starting from the **lower** note.

Look again at the intervals above.

The lower note is Eb. The higher note is G. This means we count the letter names E, F and G. Three letters, so this interval is a **third**.

When two notes are exactly the same pitch (the same position on the stave), the interval is called a **unison.**

An interval of an 8th is normally called an **octave**, or "**8ve**" for short.

You might get a question which asks you to write a note to make the named interval, something like this:

Add a note next to this note, to make the melodic interval of a 6th. The key is A major.

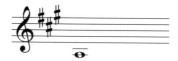

Count the letter names, starting with the given note, A. We need to count six letters: A-B-C-D-E-F. In this case, the key signature will turn the note we write into F#. Here is the answer:

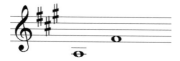

If there is no key signature, you will need to remember which sharps or flats belong in the scale of that key. In A major, there are three sharps: F#, C# and G#, so you would need to add an F# accidental to the interval of a 6th.

If the interval you have to write is a **unison** or **harmonic 2nd**, you will need to move the top note to the **side** of the lower one, otherwise they will cross over each other! They should be right next to each other, touching. A melodic unison or 2nd should have a clear gap between the two notes.

harmonic 2nd          melodic 2nd

Note: for grade 2, you will not be asked about an interval's quality, e.g. "perfect" or "major" etc.

# 14. INTERVALS EXERCISES

## EXERCISE 1

a. Draw a circle round two notes next to each other that are a 5th apart.

b. Draw a circle round two notes next to each other that are a 4th apart.

c. Draw a circle round two notes next to each other that are a 6th apart.

d. Draw a circle round two notes next to each other that are an octave apart.

## EXERCISE 2

Above each note, write another note to form the named **harmonic** interval. The key is given.

## EXERCISE 3

After each note, write a higher note to form the named **melodic** interval. The key is given.

## EXERCISE 4

After each note, write a higher note to form the named **melodic interval.** The key is given.

# 14. INTERVALS ANSWERS

EXERCISE 1

EXERCISE 2

Bb major: 5th    F major: 2nd    A major: octave    D minor: 6th

EXERCISE 3

E minor: unison    D major: 3rd    A minor: 4th    Eb major: 7th

EXERCISE 4

Eb major: 4th    D minor: 7th    Bb major: 6th    G major: octave

# 15. TRIPLETS (UK)

A "triplet" is a group of three notes played in the time of two. To look at how triplets work, we'll first look at a short rhythm in 3/4 time. Remember that in 3/4 time, one crotchet beat can be divided into two quavers. Clap the following rhythms:

One crotchet beat can also be divided into four semiquavers:

But, if we want to split the crotchet into **three** equal parts, we need to use a **triplet**.

To show a triplet, we write the notes as three quavers beamed (joined) together, and we also write "3" on the beamed side of the notes.

Look at this rhythm using triplets – if you say the words "my beautiful car" in each bar, you will get the right rhythm.

## CROTCHET TRIPLETS

Triplets don't always have to be quavers - we can make triplets out of notes of **any** length. We can split a minim up into three equal notes by writing triplet crotchets, for example:

Crotchets don't have beams, of course, so we write crotchet triplets with a bracket, with the number 3 in the middle of the longest line.

## MIXED NOTE VALUE TRIPLETS

Triplets don't always have to have **three** notes in them: the notes of the triplet just need to **add up to** three of whatever value there would normally be two of.

In 4/4 time, for example, a crotchet is worth two quavers, or three triplet quavers. This means you can make a triplet out of other note values, as long as they also add up to three quavers overall. Here are some different ways one crotchet beat can be split into triplets with different rhythms.

## Adding Bar Lines with Triplets

Adding bar lines to music with triplets can look difficult at first glance, but don't panic! Remember that you are looking at three notes in the space of two, and that they are grouped together in whole beats. Here's an example:

*Add the missing bar lines to this tune.*

The time signature is 3/4, so each bar needs to have an equivalent of three crotchet beats.

Each "3" symbol shows a triplet group. One triplet group is worth one crotchet. The quavers beamed in twos are also worth one crotchet each.

Write a "1" under each group of notes which adds up to one crotchet. (You can write "2" under the minim, and any other values which are necessary, of course!)

Then after each count of three (because this is 3/4 time), draw a bar line.

## Adding Rests with Triplets

Here's a melody which you need to add rests to, and the melody contains a triplet:

What do we need to do? We can see that there is a triplet marked with a "3" above the beamed quavers, but there are only two notes written instead of three. The star (*) shows us where the missing rest is supposed to go - in this case it's in the middle of the triplet.

The other notes in the triplet group are quavers; we've got two quavers but we need three, so the rest must have the value of a quaver. Draw the quaver rest carefully, in the place shown by the star. If you have to write a crotchet triplet rest, make sure it's inside the "triplet" brackets.

Here's the finished answer, with the quaver rest in place:

# 15. TRIPLETS (USA)

A "triplet" is a group of three notes played in the time of two. To look at how triplets work, we'll first look at a short rhythm in 3/4 time. Remember that in 3/4 time, one quarter note beat can be divided into two eighth notes. Clap the following rhythms:

One quarter note beat can also be divided into four sixteenth notes:

But, if we want to split the quarter note into **three** equal parts, we need to use a triplet.

To show a triplet, we write the notes as three eighth notes beamed (joined) together, and we also write "3" on the beamed side of the notes.

Look at this rhythm using triplets. Say the words "my beautiful car" in each measure, to get the rhythm.

## QUARTER NOTE TRIPLETS

Triplets don't always have to be eighth notes - we can make triplets out of notes of **any** length. We can split up a half note into three equal notes by writing triplet quarter notes, for example:

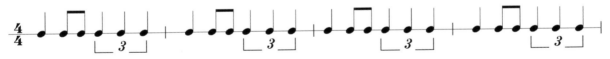

Quarter notes don't have beams, of course, so we write quarter note triplets with a bracket, with the number 3 in the middle of the longest line.

## MIXED NOTE VALUE TRIPLETS

Triplets don't always have to have **three** notes in them: the notes of the triplet just need to **add up to** three of whatever value there would normally be two of.

In 4/4 time, for example, a quarter note is worth two eighth notes, or three triplet eighth notes. This means you can make a triplet out of other note values, as long as they also add up to three eighth notes overall. Here are some different ways one quarter note beat can be split into triplets with different rhythms.

Adding bar lines to music with triplets can look difficult at first glance, but don't panic! Remember that you are looking at three notes in the space of two, and that they are grouped together in whole beats. Here's an example:

*Add the missing bar lines to this tune.*

The time signature is 3/4, so each bar needs to have an equivalent of three quarter note beats.

Each "3" symbol shows a triplet group. One triplet group is worth one quarter note. The eighth notes beamed in twos are also worth one quarter note each.

Write a "1" under each group of notes which adds up to one quarter note. (You can write "2" under the half note, and any other values which are necessary, of course!)

Then after each count of three (because this is 3/4 time), draw a bar line.

## ADDING RESTS WITH TRIPLETS

Here's a melody which you need to add rests to, and the melody contains a triplet:

What do we need to do? We can see that there is a triplet marked with a "3" above the beamed eighth notes, but there are only two notes written instead of three. The star (*) shows us where the missing rest is supposed to go - in this case it's in the middle of the triplet.

The other notes in the triplet group are eighth notes; we've got two eighth notes but we need three, so the rest must have the value of a eighth note. Draw the eighth rest carefully, in the place shown by the star. If you have to write a quarter rest as part of a triplet, make sure it's inside the "triplet" brackets.

Here's the finished answer, with the eighth rest in place:

## 15. TRIPLETS EXERCISES

### EXERCISE 1

True or false?

a. Triplets always contain three notes.

b. Triplets can be made from any types of note value, not only quavers (eighth notes)

c. Triplets are used when two notes are played in the time of three.

d. Triplets are marked with a bracket when there are no beams on the notes.

### EXERCISE 2

Add the correct rests at the places marked * to make each bar complete.

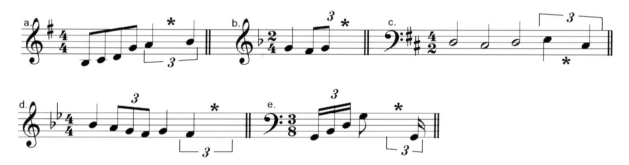

### EXERCISE 3

Add the missing bar lines to these tunes. The first bar line is given in each case.

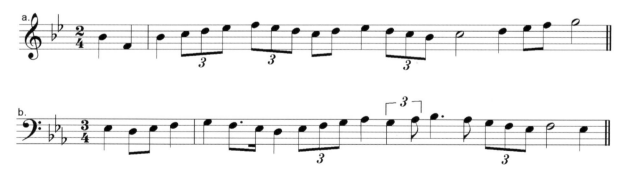

## 15. TRIPLETS ANSWERS

### EXERCISE 1

a.  False. The **value** of the notes adds up to three, but there can be any number of notes in the triplet.

b.  True.

c.  False. They are used when three notes are played in the time of two.

d.  True. (Beams are the lines that join up quavers (eighth notes) etc.)

### EXERCISE 2

### EXERCISE 2

# 16. FOREIGN TERMS

## ON FROM GRADE ONE

For Grade Two Music Theory, you have to know all the foreign musical terms and symbols which are listed for Grade One, and a few more.

In each grade of the ABRSM music theory exams there are more foreign terms to learn, but you always have to know all the terms from the earlier grades too.

## METRONOME MARKINGS

A metronome is a gadget which makes a loud, regular clicking noise. You can set the speed of the clicks. Metronomes are used so that musicians know exactly how fast to play a piece of music, and they're also useful to practise with.

Metronome markings sometimes appear above the stave, to tell you about the tempo of the music, because the Italian tempo terms are sometimes not very exact.

Metronome directions are made up of a **note symbol** and a **number**, joined together by the equals sign, like this:

This means that the tempo of the music should be about 126 crotchets (quarter notes) per **minute**. Metronome indications always tell you how many notes to play per minute. (Of course, it's best if you actually have a metronome so that you can set it to click at the speed indicated.)

Metronome markings use the note length which is the beat shown by the **time signature**.

So if the time signature is 3/2, the beat is a minim (half note), and there will be a minim (half note) shown in the metronome marking.

Time signatures with a lower number 4 have a crotchet beat (quarter note), and if the lower number is 8, the beat is a quaver (eighth note).

**Tempo**

| Italian Term | Pronunciation | English Meaning |
|---|---|---|
| Allargando | al-lar-*gan-do* | Broadening (getting a little slower and probably a little louder) |
| Grave | *grar*-vay | Very slow and solemn |
| Largo | *lar*-go | Slow and stately |
| Lento | *Len*-toe | Slowly |
| Presto | *press*-toe | Very fast |
| Ritenuto | Rit-e-*noo*-toe | Held back (also, riten., rit.) |
| Vivace | vi-*var*-chay | Lively and quickly |
| Vivo | *vee*-voe | Lively and quickly |

**Dynamics**

| Fortepiano | *for*-tay pi-*ya*-no | FP | Loud then immediately soft |
|---|---|---|---|

**Phrasing**

| | | | |
|---|---|---|---|
| Espressivo | es-press-*ee*-voe | Espress., Espr. | Expressive |
| Grazioso | grat-zee-*oh*-so | | Gracefully |
| Tenuto | ten-*oo*-toe | | Held |

**Other Terms**

| | | | |
|---|---|---|---|
| A | *a* (as in "c*a*t") | | At, To, By, For, In, In the style of |
| Al, Alla | *al, a*-la | | To the, In the manner/style of |
| Con, Col | *kon, kol* | | With |
| Dal segno | dal *sen*-yo | D.S. | From the sign |
| E, Ed | *e* (as in "bed") | | And |
| Ma | *ma* (as in "man") | | But |
| Marcia | *mar*-chia | | March |
| Meno | *men*-no | | Less |
| Molto | *mol*-toe | | Very, Much |
| Mosso, Moto | *moss-o, mo*-to | | Movement |
| Non | *nonn* | | Not |
| Piu | pi-*yu* | | More |
| Poco | *po*-ko | | Little |
| Senza | *sen*-za | | Without |
| Troppo | *tropp*-o | | Too much (*non troppo = not too much*) |

# 16. FOREIGN TERMS EXERCISES

1.      Which term means "very slow and solemn"?

a.      Allargando
b.      Grave
c.      Giocoso
d.      Rallentando


2.      Which term means "majestically"?

a.      Larghetto
b.      Senza
c.      Maestoso
d.      Grazioso


3.      What does "allargando" mean?

a.      Very fast
b.      Getting slower
c.      Very smoothly
d.      Broadening


4.      What does "dal segno" mean?

a.      To the sign
b.      From the sign
c.      To the repeat
d.      From the repeat


5.      Put these terms in order of speed from fastest to slowest: Andante, Largo, Presto, Moderato.

a.      Largo, Presto, Moderato, Andante
b.      Presto, Moderato, Andante, Largo
c.      Andante, Largo, Moderato, Presto
d.      Presto, Andante, Moderato, Largo


6.      Which word is the opposite of "meno"?

a.      Mosso
b.      Molto
c.      Piu
d.      Ma


7.      Which word means "held back"?

a.      Legato
b.      Staccato
c.      Mezzo
d.      Ritenuto


8.      Which word is the opposite of "col" ("with")?

a.      Mezzo
b.      Poco
c.      Senza
d.      Ed


9.      Which word is the odd one out?

a.      Cantabile
b.      Presto
c.      Allegro
d.      Vivace


10.     Which word means "with movement"?

a.      Con moto
b.      Mezzo forte
c.      Alla marcia
d.      Molto allegro

11. What does "ed" mean?

a. And
b. But
c. Less
d. More

12. What does "troppo" mean?

a. Three times
b. Too much
c. Trippingly
d. Very

13. Which phrase means "from the beginning"?

a. Dal segno
b. A tempo
c. Simile
d. Da capo

14. Which word can you put before "Rondo"?

a. Alla
b. Fine
c. Decrescendo
d. Senza

15. What does "grazioso" mean?

a. Freely
b. Gracefully
c. Quickly
d. Suddenly

16. The term "vivo" tells you ..................... to play something.

a. what style
b. what volume/dynamic
c. how long
d. what speed

17. The term "largo" has a similar meaning to the term:

a. Allegretto
b. Ritardando
c. Adagio
d. Accelerando

18. What does "tenuto" mean?

a. Tenderly
b. Too much
c. Held
d. Ten times

19. Which is the correct spelling of the word which means "expressively"?

a. Expressivo
b. Exspresivo
c. Espresivo
d. Espressivo

20. What does the term "senza" mean?

a. Without
b. Such
c. Because
d. With a flourish

## 16. FOREIGN TERMS ANSWERS

1. b
2. c
3. d
4. b
5. b
6. c
7. d
8. c
9. a
10. a

11. a
12. b
13. d
14. a
15. b
16. d
17. c
18. c
19. d
20. a

# 17. HANDWRITING MUSIC

It is very important that you write music in a way that is easy for others to read. Practise regularly, and look back at music you have written previously, to see if you can read it yourself!

## COMMON MISTAKES

Here are some very common mistakes that students make when writing out music - make sure you don't make them!

- Don't forget to put the bar line at the end of the extract.

- The first note of each bar is always the same distance (about 1/2 a centimetre) from the barline on its left.

- Accidentals are written on the **left-hand** side of the note head, in the line/space of the note they affect.

- Try to keep the same distance between the notes as you see in the original.

- Make sure the note stems are pointing in the right direction.

- Black note-heads must be a good solid colour - make sure you can see no white space at all inside the notehead.

- Don't make the note heads too big.

- Don't forget ties!

- Ledger lines are an extension of the stave and should be the same height apart, and slightly wider than the note heads. In this example, the B ledger line is too high, and the A ledger line is not wide enough!

## 17. HANDWRITING MUSIC EXERCISES
Copy these extracts including all details.

# GRADE 2 PRACTICE TEST | TIME LIMIT - 90 MINUTES

## EXERCISE 1

Add the missing bar lines to these two tunes. The first bar line is given in each. (10 points)

## EXERCISE 2

Write the scales as indicated. (10 points)

a. One octave of the descending major scale that uses this key signature, using semibreves (whole notes).

b. One octave of the ascending scale of D harmonic minor, using semibreves (whole notes). Use a key signature and add any other necessary accidentals.

## EXERCISE 3

a.  Give the letter name of each of the notes marked *, including the sharp or flat sign where necessary. The first answer is given. (8 points)

b.  Give the time name (e.g. crotchet or quarter-note) of the rest in the last bar. (1 point) _____

## EXERCISE 4

Add the correct clef and any necessary sharp or flat signs to each of these tonic triads. Do not use key signatures. (10 points)

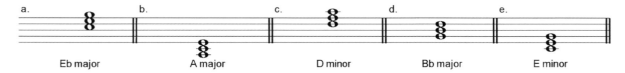

Eb major    A major    D minor    Bb major    E minor

## EXERCISE 5

Rewrite the following in notes and a rest of half the value, beginning as shown. (10 points)

## EXERCISE 6

In each of the numbered spaces, add the note or rest named below, as shown in the answer to [1]. (10 points)

[1] minim (half) **rest**

[2] F, semibreve (whole) **note**

[3] Bb, crotchet (quarter) **note**

[4] F#, minim (half) **note**

[5] F natural, dotted minim (dotted half) **note**

[6] crotchet (quarter) **rest**

## EXERCISE 7

a.   Rewrite these treble clef notes in the bass clef, keeping the pitch the same. The first answer is given. (6 points)

# EXERCISE 8

Look at this melody, adapted from a piece by Schumann, and then answer the questions below.

Answer the questions. (10 points)

a.  Give the time name (e.g. crotchet or quarter-note) of the rest in the last bar.

b.  Draw a circle round two notes next to each other which are a 6th apart.


c.  How many times does this rhythm occur?

d.  The melody is in A major. On which degree of the scale (e.g. 2nd, 3rd) does the melody begin?

e.  Answer TRUE or FALSE to this sentence:

    The time signature 2/4 means that there are two quaver (eighth-note) beats in a bar.

## GRADE 2 PRACTICE TEST ANSWERS

Total points available: 75. Pass=50, Merit=60, Distinction=65

### EXERCISE 1

### EXERCISE 2

a.

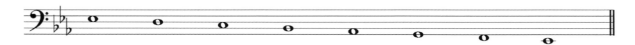

b.

### EXERCISE 3

b. Minim (half) rest.

### EXERCISE 4

## EXERCISE 5

## EXERCISE 6

## EXERCISE 7

a.

## EXERCISE 8

a.  Quaver/eighth rest

b.
c.  3 times
d.  4th
e.  False

# ANNEX

The following material was in the ABRSM Grade 2 syllabus until 1<sup>st</sup> January 2018. The topics here are no longer tested in the exam, but will prove useful for anyone with an interest in learning the craft of composition.

## COMPOSING A RHYTHM
### EXAMPLE QUESTION

Here's a question for us to work through together:

*Write a four-bar rhythm using the given opening.*

How do we start? The first thing to learn is that your 4-bar rhythm must be made up of **two phrases** - we'll call them A and B.

Phrase A is the first two bars, and phrase B is the last two.

We can think of phrase A as a "question", and phrase B as the "answer".

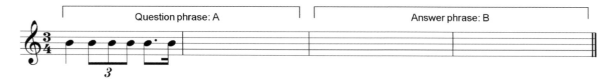

### QUESTION PHRASES

As you can see, in grade two we are actually only given **half** a question phrase (whereas in grade one you're given a complete 2-bar question). The same kind of thing in words could be something like *why do you.....?"* or *"have you ever......?"*

There are probably millions of ways to finish these questions in a sensible way, and even more ways to finish them with something meaningless!

We could ask

- Have you ever been to France?

- Why do you get up at 7 o'clock?

But it wouldn't make much sense if we asked

- Have you ever yesterday afternoon?

- Why do you rabbit mountains?

In music, the question must also make sense - **musical sense**. This means that you need to write something which fits with the first bar, and not something that is totally unconnected to it. Let's take a look at some examples.

This is ok, but not very interesting. We didn't create anything new, so we shouldn't expect many points for this! You won't normally get more than 7/10 if you copy the given opening exactly.

This doesn't fit very well because none of the note values in bar 2 appear in bar 1, so there's no connection.

This one is good - bar two uses some old material from bar one (the triplet), and some new material (the minim (half note)).

This one is also good - the note values all appear in the first bar, but we've changed the order of them. So, there is a strong connection, but it's not an exact copy.

Again, this is good because it re-uses some, but not all, of the rhythms from bar 1.

Not such a good choice - the only note value which appears in both bars is the crotchet (quarter note), but everything else is completely different. It's probably best not to include rests in your rhythm, unless they are part of the rhythm given in bar 1.

Before we think about answering the question phrase, we need to choose a completed question phrase. Let's say we finish our question phrase like this:

Look at the types of rhythm we've used **on each beat**.

We've got three types: a plain crotchet (quarter note), a triplet quaver (8th note) group and a dotted quaver/semiquaver (dotted 8th/16th) pair.

We should use mostly the same types of rhythm in our answering phrase.

The very last note of the phrase should be a reasonably long one (at least a crotchet (quarter note)), so that the rhythm sounds properly finished.

Let's take a look at some answering phrases and see which ones are any good, and why.

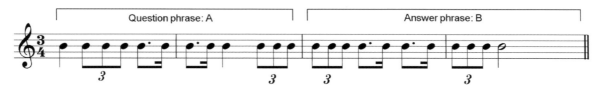

This sounds fine. We re-used some of the important rhythms, but not in the same order, and we finished on a nice long minim (half note).

This doesn't sound very good. Because we forgot about the triplets, the last two bars don't match the first two very well.

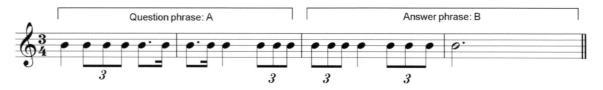

Here we forgot to re-use the dotted rhythm, and the last bar is certainly not very interesting!

This one is good - the rhythms are re-used in a different order and the final note value is a nice long end note.

This is also a good answer. The rhythms are linked, and the last note is a long enough ending note.

## COMPOSING A RHYTHM EXERCISES
Write a four-bar rhythm for each of the given openings.

1.

2.

3.

4.

5.

6.

7.

## COMPOSING A RHYTHM ANSWERS

The answers given on this page are suggested answers only, many different answers are possible.

Check you have put the right number of beats in each bar, that you have a "question" phrase
followed by an "answer" phrase, and that you have re-cycled some of the rhythms from the first bar.

1.

2.

3.

4.

5.

6.

7.